My Book About
God

"Jesus . . . said,
Suffer little children to come unto me,
and forbid them not:
for of such is the kingdom of God"
(Luke 18:16).

My Book About God

By Edith S. Witmer

Illustrated by Edith Burkholder

Rod and Staff Publishers, Inc.
P.O. Box 3, Hwy. 172
Crockett, Kentucky 41413
Telephone: (606) 522-4348

CHRISTIAN LIGHT PUBLICATIONS INC.
P.O. BOX 1212
Harrisonburg, Virginia 22803-1212
(540) 434-0768

To Ryan, Bradley, and Douglas.
With my love.

Table of Contents

Letter to Parents

Dear Parents,

This book has been written to make children aware of God, that He is as surely around them as the toys they touch. Its pages hold facts to develop in small minds the fear of God, which will be the springboard for all holiness and humility before Him in their developing years. It is offered to teach children that God loves them as infinitely as the stars of heaven reach—and further. For there is no end to God's fullness.

We have only touched gently on the subject of God's justice in punishing sin. Primarily, innocent children should first learn that God is a God of love, who teaches His children to do right, and that our lives must be humbly ordered to follow Him in obedience.

And lastly, this book is not intended to be read in one sitting. Read one poem at a time, and develop more thoughts about God as you talk to your child about the God you have learned to know and love.

What our children learn and believe about God and His holiness will determine the fruitfulness of their lives as well as their eternal destinies.

Blessings to you and your little ones!

—*Edith S. Witmer*

Thoughts to Discuss With Your Child

1. God is eternal. That means that God never needed a beginning. He always was, and He will always be. God will never die or have an end.

2. God is immutable. That means that God never changes. He always stays the same, because everything about Him is true. So there is no need for Him to change. He is always right!

3. God is omnipotent. That means that God is all-powerful. He can do anything. Nothing is too hard for God!

4. God is omniscient. That means that God knows everything. He knows the thoughts we think. He knows what will happen before it happens. And He knows what is good and right. God can answer any questions.

5. God is omnipresent. That means that God is everywhere at one time. He is with us all the time, even though our eyes cannot see Him. There is no place where God is not. No one can hide from Him. God sees everything!

6. God is righteous. That means that God will always do the right thing. When He punishes, and when He blesses, He is just and right. God cannot make a mistake in dealing with men.

7. God is faithful. That means that God is always the Friend we can count on. The Bible is full of promises of His love and care, and God keeps each one! We know that God will always be there to help us!

8. God is incomprehensible. That means that our human minds are too little to understand everything there is to know about our great God. When we get to heaven, we will be able to understand more about God. That will be wonderful!

9. God operates in simplicity. That means that even though God is grand and mighty, He does things in ways that a simple mind can grasp. The Bible is full of wonderful thoughts, but men can read it and understand God's words. Since God always does things the best way from the beginning, He can use straightforward, simple plans. God teaches his children to be simple and humble.

10. God is good. That means that God is kind and merciful. We can always depend on Him to care for us in the best way. God is our heavenly Father and our true Friend.

11. God is gracious and merciful. That means that God gives us blessings that we cannot earn, and often does not give man the bad things he deserves. God is very kind to us!

12. God is just. That means that God will always do the right thing, and that He is fair to everyone. Because God is just, He will bless good and punish evil.

13. God is love. That means that God cares about us from the very depths of His heart. Because He loves us, it is His great joy to bless us. God is the kind Father we can always trust. He holds us in His arms tenderly and lovingly!

14. God hates evil. In fact, God hates sin just as strongly as He loves good. He will also punish people who are evil, if they do not repent.

15. God is holy. That means that everything about God is pure and beautiful. God is altogether wonderful! Because He is holy, God also wants His people to be holy. We worship God because He is the almighty God who deserves our worship!

My Book About
God

God Created Me!

God made the earth, the sky, the sea,
    The stars, the burning sun,
The birds, and all the animals
    That sing, or splash or run!
But when God finished all those things,
    He made a perfect man
To tend the earth and be His friend,
    Because it was His plan.

The time came when the Lord sent me,
   A baby, soft and sweet,
To lay in my dear mother's arms,
   While Father kissed my cheek.
They were so thrilled that I had come—
   "Our gift from God is here!"

They said. "God has a purpose for
This baby, small and dear."

God thought of me and planned my life
And made me for His own.
So I belong to God, who sent
Me to the earth, on loan.

My father says God has a plan
That He sent me to do,
Until God takes me back to heaven
When my life's work is through.

So every man belongs to God,
Because He made us all.
That's why men ought to worship Him
And listen to His call.

God Knows My Name!

God knows my name! He sees my bed,
And counts each hair upon my head.
There's nothing that God does not see
Or know about my life and me!

My Name

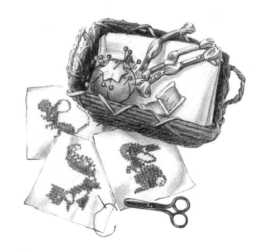

He knows that I like pumpkin pie.
　　He knows the things that make me cry.
He knows the games that I like best,
　　The things that I keep in my chest.

He sees the kind things that I do,
And when I'm bad, He sees that too.

21

When Jesus lived on earth with men,
The mothers brought their children when
    They came to hear Him preach, and pray
    To God, His Father. Gladly they
Gave Him their little ones so He
Could bless them! If it had been me,

I should have felt so safe and warm
To be in Jesus' loving arms!

23

My father says that Christ still holds
Each little lamb within His fold!

I am so glad to know that He
Still holds the children tenderly
Within His heart, and loves to share
The gentle safety of His care,

That He looks down from heav'n and smiles
Into my heart. I am His child!

God knows my name! He sees my bed,
And counts each hair upon my head.
   He loves and holds me in His care,
   At any time and everywhere!
There's nothing that God does not see
Or know about my life and me!

27

God Is Good and Kind

My Father's heart is full of love!
And His love lives to bless
All the little children with
His gift of tenderness.

28

God sends the rain to water Earth,
So I can have a drink
When I am tired and thirsty.
He sends water so our creek
Can sing and bubble on its way
Along the meadow's edge.

He waters all the great tall trees,
  The flowers by our hedge.
He sends the sun that warms my face,
  And makes our garden grow,
And scatters sunshine in the world,
  And makes the flowers glow!

He gives me my own mother dear,
Who reads my books to me.

She tucks me into my small bed,
And loves me tenderly.

My father is another gift
From God. I am so glad
To have him to protect me when
I'm feeling scared or sad.

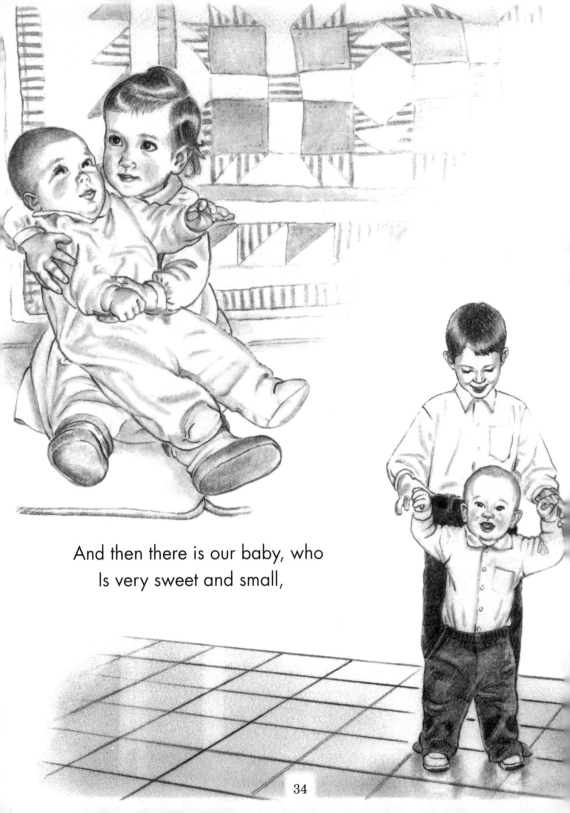

And then there is our baby, who
Is very sweet and small,

And all my bigger brothers, who
    Take me out to play ball.
They let me help them do the chores,
    And teach me things they know.
Families are true gifts from God,
    That bless us as we grow!

My father says the Bible is
  God's best gift to all men,
Because its pages tell of God.
  I like to listen when

My father reads the stories that
    Explain God and His love,
And all the lovely things
    God has in His own house, above!

My mother says we couldn't buy
A joyful heart. But we
Can have the gift because God wants
Us to live happily.

It is His joy to bless us with
    Good things that are the best!
Our Father's heart is good and kind,
    And that's why we are blessed!

God Sees Me

God watches me with eyes that see
Everything there is of me.

40

He sees when I smile and obey,
Or when I fuss to get my way.

God sees the Earth, a big round ball.
Yet He sees everything that's small—
    Each tiny flower, my kitten, soft,
    And children playing in the loft.

He never tires or goes to bed,
But always watches me instead.
   In every place, at any time,
   His eyes see everything, while mine
Can only see the little space
That is in front of my small face.

God's eyes are kind and filled with love.
From His own throne, in heaven above,
He watches every girl and boy,
They bring to His kind heart great joy!

45

God watches me with eyes that see
Everything there is of me,
And He smiles! How glad I am
That I am His own little lamb!

God Is Everywhere!

I can only be one place,
   But God is everywhere!
He's at my house. He's in the barn.
   He's at the neighbor's where
My father's working.
   And I know that He must also be
In other states where my friends live.
   He's everywhere, you see!

Illinois

Indiana

Ohio

He's also in each country that
Is on Earth—every place!

And then, of course, He's with the stars
That move around in space.

There is no place God cannot be!
He's each place all the time.
How great He is! I am so glad
That I can call Him mine.

God is a Spirit, Mother says,
While I can only stay
Inside my body, at one place.
With God, it's not that way.

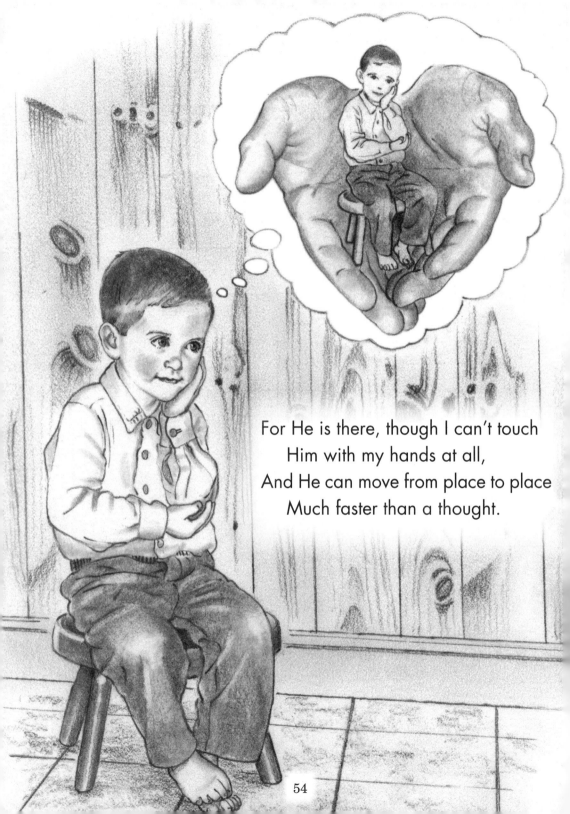

For He is there, though I can't touch
Him with my hands at all,
And He can move from place to place
Much faster than a thought.

54

And yet He's every place at once!
How great our God must be
To share His Person everywhere,
And not need a body.

My father said that God can use
    A body if He likes.
He has a throne, in heav'n, His home,
    To sit on. And He rides

Across the heavens in the clouds.
I am so glad to know
That I cannot go any place
That my great God can't go!

God Is Great!

God made the earth by speaking words!
  And He created light
By simply telling it to come—
  And chased away the night!

From nothing, God made something good.
And then His hands formed man
To be His friend and talk with Him.
God's greater than I am!

59

I cannot tell a tree to grow,
Or make a mud pie live.
But God is great! And His kind heart
Just loves to give and give!

My mother said God never has
A birthday. For He's been,
With no beginning, and that He
Will never have an end.

Though we cannot explain that fact,
It is enough to know
That it is true and clearly right—
Because our God said so!

God knows the things that happen
Before they can come to pass,
Because His heart and mind know all.
To Him it is no task!

He knows the things that I will do
When I become a man,
Before I'll ever do them! God
Is great and wise. He can

Do anything and everything!
And His mind can explain
The biggest questions people ask,
Because He is our King!

There is no limit to the things
     That my great God can do!
He's good and kind! He's strong and wise,
     And all He says is true!

God Loves Me

God loves me more than words can say!
It is His gift. It is His way
    To bless me with a love so wide
    That there would be no place to hide

Where His love is not. Everywhere
The Lord shows tokens of His care,
And everyday He watches me,
To love and bless me tenderly.

For like a shepherd, Jesus keeps
The little lambs and full-grown sheep
Within His sheepfold. Someday He
Will take us to His house to be

With Him where there will be no night,
No sin, no crying, where the light
   Will be His Presence, and pure love
   Makes everything a joy, above!

The great, huge ocean could not hold
All of God's love! Nor could the gold

Of all earth's treasure ever buy
One drop of it. Yet God, on high,
Stoops down and smiles to bless and touch
Our hearts that need His love, so much!

For like a blanket, soft and warm,
God's love enfolds me, and His arm
Surrounds me tenderly to share
The strong protection of His care!
God loves me more than words can say!
I thank Him for this gift each day!

God Hates Sin

The Lord hates sin. So I won't do
  Things that I know are bad.
For they would spoil a happy day
  And make God's kind heart sad.

My father says there is no sin
 In heaven, at God's home,
That only pure and lovely things
 Can come before God's throne.

He says that when I obey
    And do the things I should,
I'm pleasing God. For it's God's plan
    That children should be good

And do the things their parents teach
 Them to do every day.
That means God gave me parents, dear,
 To teach me His true way.

81

My father says that our whole house
    Will gladly serve the Lord,
Like Joshua in Bible times.
    We want God's best reward!

The Lord hates sin. So I won't do
Things that I know are bad.
I'll listen to my parents! That
Will make God's pure heart glad!

God Is Holy and Unchangeable

The Lord is holy. He will do
    Things that are good and right.
He cannot sin or do wrong things.
    Instead, He is the Light
That shines into our world to bring
    True joy and happiness.
For He is good and kind to us,
    And His heart loves to bless.

He wants folks not to do bad things,
But rather to obey
His Word, the Bible, and to do
His holy will each day.

85

When I draw pictures, I erase
My smudgy, poor mistakes,

And then I try again to draw
  The things I want to make.
I change because I did things wrong
  To start with. But the Lord
Will only do things perfectly,
  As He says in His Word.

God never changes. But he stays
    The same from year to year.
His thoughts are true and always right.
    So we need never fear
That He will make the least mistake,
    For what He does is best!
So people can depend on God
    And come to Him for rest.

For He will do what's good and right,
So there's no need to change!
I'm glad that God is holy, that
He always is the same!

We Worship God

Since God is great, we bow to pray
And thank Him for our food each day.
He made us, and He gives us food
Because His heart is kind and good.

We go to church to pray, and sing
To His great name. For everything
Should praise the Lord! We kneel to pray
Because we're small, and made from clay,
While God, who made the sun and stars,
Is so much greater than we are!

Since God is wise and knows what's best,
We do what He says and are blest!

And His Word tells me to obey
My loving parents. I'm glad they
Teach me to worship God. For He
Is so much mightier than me!